How the Rabbit Caught the Tiger

by Patricia Griffith
illustrated by Pat Doyle

Practice Decodable 91

McGraw Hill Education

Bothell, WA • Chicago, IL • Columbus, OH • New York, NY

MHEonline.com

Send all inquiries to:
McGraw-Hill Education
8787 Orion Place
Columbus, OH 43240

ISBN: 978-0-02-145143-2
MHID: 0-02-145143-5

Printed in China.

8 9 10 11 12 DSS 27 26 25 24 23

The Rabbit and the Tiger

One winter's eve, a mighty and hungry tiger trapped a tiny rabbit.

"Do not eat me!" cried the rabbit.

"I am too small to make a good meal. If you let me go, I will show you how to catch all the fish you can eat."

The tiger was greedy. His hunger was bigger than his brain. "Show me now, or I will eat you, little rabbit!" he roared. Then he let the rabbit go.

The rabbit led the tiger down to a river. The rabbit told the tiger, "Put your tail in the water."

"Now wait all night. Fish will grab your tail. Soon your tail will grow heavy. Then you can take it out and eat all the fish!"

"I'll stay close by," whispered the rabbit. "I will let you know when you have caught plenty of fish."

The rabbit climbed up the riverbank and sat down across from the tiger.

The tiger put his tail into the river. He waited and waited. It grew cold and dark.

The Rabbit's Trick

"Is your tail getting heavy?" called the rabbit.

"Yes!" replied the tiger. "I must be catching lots of fish! Do you think I ought to take my tail out now?"

"No!" cried the rabbit. "If you wait until morning, you will have more fish to eat!"

The greedy tiger waited longer. It grew colder and colder. His tail grew heavier.

Finally the sun came up. The tiger's tail felt quite heavy. "It is time!" called the tiger. "I am getting my fish out now!"

The tiger tugged and tugged, but his tail did not come out. It was frozen in solid ice!

"I'm going to get you, little rabbit!" roared the tiger. But he could not budge at all.

The rabbit giggled and scampered away. He had tricked a mighty tiger!